Carlo Cardinal Martini

# WOMEN
# AND
# RECONCILIATION

VERITAS

Published 1987 by
Veritas Publications
7-8 Lower Abbey Street
Dublin 1

Italian language edition published 1985 by
Edizioni Piemme
15033 Casale Monferrato
Italy

ISBN 0 86217 239 X

Translation: Luke Griffin
Cover design: Eddie McManus
Typesetting: Printset & Design Ltd, Dublin
Printed in the Republic of Ireland by
Mount Salus Press Ltd, Dublin

# CONTENTS

# 1
# ATTENTIVENESS

# ATTENTIVENESS

*(Luke 1: 26-35)*
*In the sixth month the angel Gabriel was sent from God to a city of Galilee named Nazareth, to a virgin betrothed to a man whose name was Joseph, of the house of David; and the virgin's name was Mary. And he came to her and said 'Hail, full of grace, the Lord is with you'. But she was greatly troubled at the saying, and considered in her mind what sort of greeting this might be. And the angel said to her, 'Do not be afraid, Mary, for you have found favour with God. And behold you will conceive in your womb and bear a son, and you shall call his name Jesus. He will be great, and will be called the Son of the Most High; and the Lord God will give to him the throne of his father David. And he will reign over the house of Jacob for ever; and of his Kingdom there will be no end'.*
*And Mary said to the angel, How can this be, since I have no husband?'*
*And the angel said to her, 'The Holy Spirit will come upon you, and the power of the Most High will overshadow you; therefore the child to be born will be called holy, the Son of God.'*

*(John 2: 1-5)*
*On the third day there was a marriage at Cana in Galilee, and the mother of Jesus was there; Jesus was invited to the marriage with his disciples. When the wine failed, the mother of Jesus said to him, 'They have no wine'. And Jesus said to her, 'O woman, what have you to do with me'. My hour has not yet come' His mother said to the servants, 'Do whatever he tells you'.*

**Introduction**

I thank you, Lord Jesus, for once again bringing us together to contemplate your Word which is great and which we

9

will not cease to contemplate on this earth. We, O Lord, wish to learn to continue to contemplate your Word until that day when we shall contemplate you face to face for eternity.

I warmly welcome each of you: those I already know; those here for the first time and those I have met during parish visitations. Our study of the Word of God, under the heading of reconciliation, will in part continue our earlier themes. Last year we had just completed the (diocesan) synod and this year we are preparing for the meeting of the Italian dioceses which will take place in Loreto.

This year we will examine the notion of reconciliation, not in the abstract but rather in so far as it applies to the human community and in particular to women. It is the Lord himself who invites us to deeper reflection on the role and mission of woman as the focal point of so many problems afflicting our society.

We wish to come to a contemplative reflection on a crucial issue, to speak in an objective and transcendental way about reconciliation: woman as the bearer of strengths and abilities, which are for all, men and women, though expressed more clearly in some than in others and most notably in Mary.

## The woman of reconciliation
We will contemplate Mary in her uniqueness — as feminine, as woman, as universal, as believer.

> Mary, you know that we are unable to speak of you; you are beyond our comprehension. We ask you to speak to us yourself; speak to our hearts in that interior language which even we can understand when you speak to us.

We will go on to discover the signs worked by the Spirit in the woman, Mary, and in the other women of the Gospel. They are for us examples of reconciliation, of openness and immediacy — well-springs of peace.

It may be useful to recall the valuable distinction drawn by Hans Urs von Balthasar between the 'petrine principle' and the

10

'marian principle' in the Church. The petrine principle guides the structures, the organisation and functions of the Church and works through the hierarchy and ministers of the Church. The marian principle guides the Church in communion, in welcoming and in the growth of love.

I would hope to underline the marian principle at work in the Church; Mary is *par excellence* the woman of reconciliation who raises up in the Church striking figures of reconciliation, making us men and women of reconciliation.

Briefly then, this is the scope of our series of reflections which will, of course, always have passages from the Scriptures as their starting point. I will be inviting you to look at the overall meaning of the Gospel extracts, going beyond the particulars that make them up.

Come next June our prayer meetings will have been going on for five years. It is my belief that the time has now come for you to share this experience with others at local level and at wider levels.


## Invitation to contemplation:
## The Annunciation and the Wedding Feast at Cana

*a)   The Annunciation: attentiveness to the divine dimension*
The account of the Annunciation invites us to contemplate the mystery of the appearance of a heavenly messenger to Mary and her reaction to the angel. What does Mary do? She listens, she is alert, she questions. It is the perfect attitude of dialogue — at once instinctive, courteous and attentive. It is a perfect response to a totally new, unforeseen, quite unexpected situation. If we had been in her place, would we not have gone from terror to paralysis to a demand for proof? We would have been overcome either by fear or by over-excitement, either of which would have led us astray.

> Mary, we contemplate you here in your simplicity, sensitivity, discretion, and in your strength without subservience; you want to know, to see things clearly, and at the same time to love and embrace the truth.

11

*b)*   *The Wedding Feast at Cana: attentiveness to the human dimension*
Let us now look at Mary during the wedding feast at Cana. What
does she do? She joins in the feast, helps out, eats, drinks, joins
in conversation, but all the while with a certain detachment as
she observes things and grasps their meaning. This attitude of
detached, discreet attention to what was happening enabled her
to notice something that escaped the attention of others: the wine
had run out. Mary is attentive to the human dimension, to what
is going on around her, to persons and to things.

I invite you to enter personally into these gospel scenes in their
entirety, whilst trying to grasp the mystery of Mary's *attentiveness*:
in the first scene to the angel (the divine dimension of life), in
the second to the banquet, to people, to her friends (the human
dimension of existence).


## Attentiveness — a reflection

We could now reflect for a moment on the attitude which I have
been calling 'attentiveness'; it characterises Mary's approach
to the divine, as well as to the simple things in life.

Attentiveness is a vigilant attitude towards others; it is a clear-
sightedness, a readiness to notice signs of suffering around us
and a willingness to get involved. Lack of attentiveness, on the
other hand, is the absence of this vigilance: it is the narrowness
of being caught up in ourselves; it means talking to a sick person
about our affairs but not noticing that he is perspiring, that he
needs a glass of water. Lack of attentiveness results in a cutting
remark, heedless of the hurt that it could do to one of our
listeners; in a word, it is a lack of awareness of what happens
to others.

Attentiveness means that our hearts miss a beat at any lack
of courtesy, regard or respect for others. For example: if we are
driving a car or a motor-cycle we stop before the zebra crossing;
we do not zig-zag around the pedestrian as if he or she were
a skittle. Attentiveness means that we do not smoke if it disturbs
others. It means knowing how to stand back from ourselves and
from the events around us to get a more objective view of what
is really at stake.

12

Attentiveness is, therefore, real love; it is a love which is courteous, disinterested and foreseeing. Again, attentiveness is what a mother feels towards the child growing in her womb, or what the father feels towards his child who is playing in the front garden; it is the attitude of the courteous host who is thoughtful but not intrusive.

Attentiveness is a human quality which is a necessary precondition for all spiritual advancement. Two years ago in our meetings here in the Cathedral the idea came to me to reflect on attentiveness when we were talking about great conversion stories, in this case, that of Simone Weil. She was a woman of the Jewish faith who had marvellous insights into the mystery of God. She reached, as it were, the threshold of Christianity, but did not have the courage to take the final step.

Simone Weil contrasts attentiveness and will. The faculty of will — the desire to do and to succeed — tends to make us tense. Attentiveness, on the other hand is, at the highest level, prayer, faith and love. Certain of our efforts, according to Simone Weil, produce an effect which is the opposite to what we desire: where we keep pushing with our will we ought, on the contrary, to have concentrated on listening, on attentiveness and love. Thus there arises so much bitterness, so much false asceticism and self-denial which are in reality a thinly disguised form of egoism.

It was not by chance that I invited you to meditate on this subject: I know only too well how difficult it is to put words on this reality. In and with Mary let us be attentive; this means listening to the continuous and irresistible urgings of the Holy Spirit who is within. He is the source of the power of that love which reconciles the universe.

> Lord, grant that we may understand these truths which are basic to more simple human relations. We are so frequently found wanting and are only now and then aware of these truths.

## Accountability
We are now at the third phase of our meditation. We have to

be accountable in the light of the truths we have been contemplating.

*a)    What is it in my life that impedes that attentiveness so evident in Mary?*
Some answers may come readily. All forms of greed and self-indulgence of body and mind are opposed to attentiveness: of the body, gluttony; of the senses, sensuality; of the heart, rigid desires, distress, bitterness, rancour. When we are choked by gluttony, ambition, sensuality, bitterness, rancour, dislikes, by being closed to people, by our dependence to the point of slavery on events or things, our life is no longer lived normally. It is very trying to live our lives while coping with these blockages which are deeply rooted in our consciousness.

> Jesus, grant that I may understand how my body and my heart are full of false tensions that shut out attentiveness and prevent me from really living.

Many destructive conflicts are born of lack of attentiveness. A short time ago I was struck by the statements of two young prisoners, ex-terrorists, who said in all truth and simplicity: 'we went astray completely because of our attachment to an ideology in whose name we perpetrated stupidities, losing sight of persons, not even being aware of their existence.' They added that they were further encouraged to understand the Church by coming to know of voluntary Christian groups; they were amazed at how these groups were attentive to persons in a one-to-one relationship.

*b)    What is it, for me, that favours an attitude of attentiveness?*
Mary's attitude, this lived state of grace which is psycho-spiritual, manifested in a genuine presence to reality, not in alienation but in alert courteous and humble service.

We should not be afraid to mention simple things that facilitate attentiveness (which includes being relaxed and detached) as well as alertness, spiritual agility, inner freedom, a capacity to be enthused by all things beautiful, and a capacity to make calm, mature judgements avoiding rashness.

We should examine our experiences and discover what

facilitates this basic attitude which is at the root of all reconciliation and of all peace. In my own case a number of things spring to mind; music (what kind of music facilitates attentiveness and detachment?), silence, song, the mountains, fasting, the rosary, solitude, the company of a few people who create an easy atmosphere, contemplation of the Gospels.

All of us will surely discover, in our own experiences, those realities which help us to enter this grace-filled state of being in which we can accomplish great things. This is the state of grace of which Jesus speaks when he says: 'You are amazed at these things but you will see greater and you will do even greater.' (Cf. *Jn 1:50;14:12*)

Attentiveness is a grace that is sought after with appropriate means: these are not only in stretching the spirit but more in insistent prayer, in wisdom with regard to what pertains to the body, and in experience.

*c)   Towards whom am I to show attentiveness in the coming days?*
The most beautiful friendships are weakened and destroyed by various forms of inattentiveness. Misunderstandings arise in families, between engaged couples, between husband and wife. But gestures of attentiveness reconcile and heal and weave bonds of peace!

This year we mark the 1600th anniversary of the arrival of St Augustine in Milan. When the Saint who was not yet a believer describes how he came to know Ambrose, he tells us that he was struck by his affability and his attentiveness, above all by the fact that Ambrose spoke at length about Monica, Augustine's mother; and Augustine found in his words a tangible fraternity. From the encounter began his study of the Word of God and eventually came his conversion.

> Grant, Lord, that we may be able to contemplate the mystery of Mary's attentiveness in the company of St Ambrose who treated the faltering Augustine with care and attentiveness. Grant that we may be a sign for others and may each one of us, myself first, this very evening ask for pardon for our lack of attentiveness which may have hurt or prevented others from a deeper quest for you.

# 2
# PRACTICALITY

# PRACTICALITY

(*Luke 1:36-45*)
*Behold, your kinswoman Elizabeth in her old age has also conceived a
son; and this is the sixth month with her who was called barren. For with
God nothing will be impossible. And Mary said 'Behold, I am the
handmaid of the Lord; let it be to me according to your word'. And the
angel departed from her.*

*In those days Mary arose and went with haste into the hill country,
to a city of Judah and she entered the house of Zechariah and greeted
Elizabeth. And when Elizabeth heard the greeting of Mary, the babe leaped
in her womb; and Elizabeth was filled with a loud cry, 'Blessed are you
among women, and blessed is the fruit of your womb! And why is this
granted me, that the woman of my Lord should come to me? For behold,
when the voice of your greeting came to my ears, the babe in my womb
leaped for joy. And blessed is she who believed that there would be a
fulfilment of what was spoken to her from the Lord'!*

(*Luke 2:6-7*)
*While they were there, the time came for her to be delivered. And she gave
birth to her first-born son and wrapped him in swaddling clothes, and
laid him in a manger, because there was no room for them in the inn.*

You may well ask yourselves why I have called this reflection
'practicality'. It has its origin in the prayer I addressed last year
to St Charles Borromeo on the occasion of the fourth centenary
of his death. I wrote: 'I am fascinated and at the same time
disquieted, St Charles, by your ability to translate pastoral ideas
into practical action' (cf. first part of *A Letter to St Charles*).
Referring to various pastoral letters I tried to discover what could
be the practical outcome of the proposed programme. 'The

invitation to place the Eucharist at the centre of the life and mission of the Church', I wrote, 'was strongly proclaimed during the Eucharistic Congress. But it has not yet found practical expression.' We would find it hard to pinpoint practical examples of adult catechesis, the theme of the mission.

Thus the theme of 'practicality' arose from my dialogue with St Charles about my own spiritual journey and the future path for the diocese. It is evident that this theme covers all aspects of personal and social life.

## The opposite of practicality

In order to understand better what we mean by practicality it may help to look at its opposite.

Indulging in day-dreams is the opposite of practicality. It is good that we should dream, but we should not indulge in dreams that do not lead to action. St James warns us: 'Be doers of the word, and not hearers only, deceiving yourselves. (*Jm 1:22*) To lack practicality is to deceive ourselves.

All those short-lived enthusiasms in which we indulge are a lack of practicality. Jesus speaks of these in his parable of the sower. The seed that falls on stony ground represents those who hear the word with joy, they believe for a while and rejoice but in the moment of trial they fall away.

To allow ourselves to be guided by an ideology — a form of false practicality — is to lack real practicality. We bend our experiences to suit an arbitrary idea of reality and in its name we neglect the attentiveness due to people and to events around us.

The gap between the word and the deed, between listening and doing and between the promise and its fulfilment is a lack of practicality. The gap, like a cancer, eats away at our lives. Biblically we could characterise it as the gap between the eye, the ear, the heart and the hand: the eye is attentiveness, the ear is listening, the heart is the decision and the hand is practicality — action. If the eye, the ear, the heart and the hand each goes its own way our life becomes incoherent, frustrated and inconclusive. It is the fundamental trauma of an alienated existence.

It goes without saying that practicality is not the same as being busy, on the move, plugging voids and empty spaces with words. This would be pure agitation, neurosis.


## Mary's practicality

Practicality lies in the proper relationships between hearing, deciding and acting; it is the proper balance between ear and eye, heart and hands.

If we re-read the biblical text we can see how Mary was practical. In the first text Mary listens, decides and acts (Lk 1:36-45).

First of all she *listens*: practicality is the ability to listen and to reflect.

What does Mary hear? A fact: 'Elizabeth, your kinswoman, has in her old age conceived a son and this is the sixth month. . ..' But not only does she hear of the event but she also grasps its meaning. 'Nothing is impossible to God'. With her ears Mary receives a fact and its deeper meaning; this is really what listening is about.

In the second instance Mary *decides*. She has reflected, she has listened — indeed from Luke's text we know that she asked herself what was the meaning of the way she had been greeted — and then she asks the angel 'How shall this come about?' Having listened more carefully and reflected more deeply, she decides: 'Behold the handmaid of the Lord, be it done unto me according to thy word.'

This decision by 'the heart' is at the very root of practicality; it is, in fact, its focal point. Practicality is, therefore, not just any sort of doing; it is a submission to truth, a response to a call, the expression in daily life of what has been understood.

I have always been impressed by what happened during Thomas More's last journey. He was being led along the Thames to the Tower of London, where he was to be tortured and eventually killed, when suddenly he shattered the night silence and exclaimed 'I have decided!' What did he decide at just that moment? Obviously his arrest by the King's emissaries disturbed and dismayed him. However, during the final journey his long reflection prior to his arrest came to fruition; he reached the moment of choice and he decided to go the whole way in defence of the purity of his faith and of his personal honesty. Practicality burst forth in the moment when he passed from choice to decision.

In the third instance Mary *acts*. She undertook the journey and reached, in haste, the city of Judah. It is very interesting to reflect on the strange nature of this journey. Nobody knew about Elizabeth and we can be sure that Mary's friends and relatives would have been critical of her undertaking. 'What has come over you, going off like this just before your wedding?' 'What about the wedding dress?' And then, no doubt, the whispering — what is a young girl in her situation doing, going off like this, what does she want, what is she up to. . .?

However, Mary is quite clear in her heart about what she wants and her practicality does not allow her to be stopped by anyone or anything. The evangelist notes, 'she went in haste'; St Ambrose uses an almost untranslatable Latin phrase, *'nescit tarda molimina Spiritus Sancti gratia'* ('delayed efforts are foreign to the grace of the Holy Spirit').

It is as if, once the deed has been announced, the decision taken in the depths of the heart, action must follow; otherwise the reality would decay within us. This is true even of small things: a letter which we should write, a difficult visit that we ought to make, an initiative that weighs on us, a job which we have decided to do but which we continue to postpone.

Postponements and delays wear us out, weigh us down, inwardly corrupt us from the inside.

> O Mary, you unify human nature with itself for you discovered that division and distraction are the worms that insidiously gnaw away at our hearts.

The person who is not practical is divided, torn by secret fears. The first need for reconciliation is then **within** each one of us. We need to reconcile the eye and the ear with the heart and the hand, to reconcile what is understood with what is done. We need to realise the dangers of leaving undone what is to be done, what is right and true.

Mary, put harmony in our lives. Unify in us our minds, our hearts and our actions.

In the second extract from Luke there is a very short description:

> While they were there, the time came for her to be delivered. And she gave birth to her first-born son and wrapped him in swaddling cloths and laid him in a manger, because there was no place for them in the inn. (2:6-7)

'She gave birth to her first-born son' — if we had written this, could we have resisted emotional comment? 'She rejoiced as a mother does on seeing her newborn.' Or again we might be tempted into making a comment of a religious nature — 'She adored him, she venerated him.' Or even one of a psychological nature — 'She relaxed now that the tension was past'. Finally perhaps, we might have added a social comment — 'She was sad at the thought that she gave birth to her son in a stable, she was sorry for herself, for her isolated and sad situation.'

Luke, however, states that she covered her son with swaddling cloths and placed him in a manger. She did everything practical that could be done in the circumstances. There was no futile speculation as to what might have been; she went ahead and did the corrct and urgent things that were an adequate response to the experience she was living.

We should underline the importance of the phrase 'she wrapped him in swaddling cloths' for the rest of the Lucan account. I have wondered for a long time why the sign given by the angel to the shepherds should have been 'you will find him wrapped in swaddling cloths and laid in a manger'. The insistence on the cloths and the manger probably signifies the following: The manger on the one hand points to a child who was left, abandoned, cared for by nobody, a foundling; on the other hand the cloths point to a child who is lovingly cared for, the object of love, who has been given maximum attention in the midst of absolute privation. In this way it becomes an unambiguous sign which guides the shepherds to the one whom they seek.

## Practicality and femininity

In the light of what we said about Mary we should consider the effective practicality in feminine experience or, more precisely, consider that effective practicality which, although it is not by any means exclusive to women, is often very evident in them. It is an ability to understand almost by intuition what should be done *here and now;* it is manifest in a distrust of inconclusive and abstract arguments; it is a feeling for people, for relationships, for the here and now.

This consideration leads us to conclude that any values that exist in the world are practical and concrete because being practical and concrete means being lovingly attentive in the highest possible degree to the values that are realisable in a given situation.

I would like to read a few lines from a letter I received some time ago which is an example of practicality: 'The experience of our Thursday (prayer) meetings in the cathedral marked the beginning of my missionary vocation. During those high points of my life I gained a lived experience of Christ in our midst.'

Thanks be to God, I know that this is not the only person who, because of our experience of prayer over the past few years, has chosen a life of practical dedication.

I am reminded that our answer to vocation is an extremely practical answer. It is a decisive choice of what has matured in our hearts. I would like to invite you to pray along with me for all those who, because of our Thursday meetings, have taken decisive and practical options for good in their lives.


## Questions for us

*First question:* what elements of practicality are missing from my life? Where do I notice most a hiatus between eye, ear, heart and hand, between promises and fulfilment, between the real and the ideal, between faith and life? More specifically, what are the inconsistencies in my life for which I most blame myself, or for which others blame me? What is the weak point of my practicality? Perhaps it is the eyes — because I am given to daydreams and am carried away, but do not come to a conclusion?

24

Or perhaps it is my heart — are my decisions weak, without ever reaching a point where I decide precisely what I want? Or perhaps my hands? Perhaps I am lazy; even though I decide I do not act. Why do I not act?

*Second question:* In the area of practicality what are the strong points, or the strong point, on which I should build? If I am of a contemplative temperament, my strength will perhaps be in the eye and the mind; I should then ask how my contemplation can be extended towards decision and action. If I am of an affective temperament, my strength will lie in my heart; I would then need to deepen my affectivity to make it practical. If I am active by temperament, my strength will lie in my hands; I would then have to see how my hands should be rooted in my mind and in my heart, so that all I do is not the result of restlessness or agitation, but rather the fruit of thoughtful and practical choices.

We should endeavour to make these questions operative in our lives. We should pinpoint for ourselves the times and situations during the day when we fall short, when others might rightly blame us.

Those who are priests or otherwise engaged in pastoral work might ask themselves: Why are we so often accused of preaching that lacks practicality?

## Practicality, politics and poverty

Finally, I would like to underline the relationship between practicality, poverty and politics. Here I am concerned with the ways forward for the ecclesial and human communities: both are searching for reconciliation involving all their strengths, which are at times overbearing because they are not interrelated.

a) Christian practicality is expressed in a special way in relation to the poor, and it is evident in the care for the poor of our time. Here is where the practicality of the community is to be expressed, not in a vague, but rather in a special way that examines the situation and takes up commitment again after a lapse.

b) Action on behalf of the poor is not practical if there is no sharing and if it is not expressed publicly, mobilising the political community at all levels and to the widest possible extent. This mobilisation for justice is to ensure that all receive their just share — of food, work and dignity — beginning with those who are least well-off and who therefore experience the greatest difficulty. If this is not done, action on behalf of the poor is not practical or concrete; it may indeed remain illusory, an exercise in good intentions, or even in self-satisfaction.

c) Faced with the extraordinary needs of our time (I think of the throngs who are marginalised and famine-stricken), we are struck by the urgent necessity of unifying in ourselves and in our communities the public aspects of action in favour of the poor (without which we cannot effectively face up to social and economic marginalisation) along with the personal aspects of human contact, of one-to-one relationships, of the relationship of Mary to Elizabeth, of Mary to her child.

If we do not achieve personal relationships with those in need there will be no genuinely human solutions to the manifold poverty of people today. On the other hand if we cannot achieve a more reasonable use of power, geared towards a more just social and economic order, the community will remain ineffectual in the exercise of practical and concrete love towards the needy. As a consequence we will have, not a genuine community, but groups divided among themselves, vainly looking for an escape from the barrenness of their own mediocrity.

The contemplation of Mary's practicality, it seems to me, gives rise to these considerations. It would be great if, together with ecclesial vocations, vocations to politics would also mature among us. Both of these would be a call to the service of justice and of the most poor; each in its own way would be an expression of a practical response to the Word of God.

O Mary, you know our weakness, you know how very hard it is for us to make all these things practical. Grant us a sense of urgency and immediacy, a sense of the presence of good and grant that through our attention to the practical we may discover your son, Jesus, in our midst.

# 3
# LISTENING

# LISTENING

*(Luke 10: 38-42)*
*Now as they went on their way, he entered a village; and a woman named Martha received him into her house. And she had a sister called Mary who sat at the Lord's feet and listened to his teaching. But Martha was distracted with much serving; and she went to him and said, 'Lord, do you not care that my sister has left me to serve alone? Tell her then to help me' But the Lord answered her, 'Martha, Martha, you are anxious and troubled about many things; one thing is needful. Mary has chosen the good portion which shall not be taken away from her'.*

*(Luke 2: 18-19, 51-52)*
*And all who heard it wondered at what the shepherds told them. But Mary kept all these things, pondering them in her heart.*
*And he went down with them and came to Nazareth, and was obedient to them; and his mother kept all these things in her heart.*
*And Jesus increased in wisdom and in stature and in favour with God and man.*

For those of you who have come for the first time let me remind you that the theme of our meetings is 'the woman of reconciliation'. We are examining then the problem of reconciliation with, however, a particular emphasis: God gives each one of us the capacity for reconciliation, one which is more strikingly present in the mystery of woman and in a very singular way in Mary, the woman of reconciliation *par excellence*.

We want to meditate on some of the mysteries of Mary: contemplating her singularity as Mary, her femininity as woman, her universality as believer. Thus we wish to discover the Spirit's action in her which gives to the world a thrust towards openness, immediacy and reconciliation.

## The capacity to listen

This evening we will concentrate on *listening*. A lot could be said about this key word which runs right through the tradition of the Hebrew people. 'Listen, O Israel.' It will be more helpful, perhaps, for us to read the text of Luke which describes the ability to listen in the very feminine figure of Mary of Bethany, who is so like Mary of Nazareth.

The context of the episode should be noted. Jesus is on a journey towards Jerusalem. 'As they went their way he entered a village . . .' His way leads him to Jerusalem and *this,* his way, it is a symbol too of our life of faith. I recall quite clearly that I began to make my way to Milan five years ago, but I keep in mind the goal that is really 'Jerusalem'.

As he was travelling to the Holy City we find the episode of Mary of Bethany offering hospitality to Jesus. The text stresses the importance of listening to the Word. In Luke's gospel this passage follows immediately after the account of another journey, one from Jerusalem to Jericho. This last is the parable of the Good Samaritan and it ends with the words, 'go and do likewise', that is, 'act, move, get working'. But in order that this 'doing' is not just any activity, but one which arises from deep within, the evangelist immediately adds the narrative about Mary's listening.

We can see these two passages as forming one instruction. The passage about the Good Samaritan and the one about Mary listening to Jesus are deliberately placed together so that we can see the unity between doing and listening. Indeed, in chapter 11 verse 28 Jesus says, 'Blessed are those who hear the Word and do it'. We achieve our fullness through listening to the Word and at the same time doing it.

The climax of this story about Mary of Bethany is the saying of Jesus: 'Mary has chosen the better part.' There is, though, a promise which is the context of the account: 'Mary sat at the feet of Jesus . . . listened to his teaching.' I would like to pause here and try to capture the depth of this description.

'Grant Lord, that we too may sit at your feet so that we might understand the richness and the intensity of this action.'

### 'She sat at the feet of Jesus'

This is a technical expression which means being someone's disciple, choosing someone to be a master. In the Acts of the Apostles, chapter 22, where Paul gives an account of his infancy and early education, the literal translation of the text is 'I was educated *at the feet* of Gamaliel'. Mary, therefore, makes herself a disciple of Jesus; she publicly declares that she belongs to his school together with the Twelve.

It is, therefore, easy to understand the scandal and the shock provoked by this incident. Mary, a woman, dares to associate with the most intimate disciples of Jesus, becoming a disciple herself.

We should try to imagine the murmurings of the people: Why is the woman joining a school of theology instead of staying in the kitchen? Who does she think she is? What is she up to? What kind of ambitions does she have? There is a certain tension in the atmosphere which is expressed by Martha's words.

Mary, who has chosen the Lord of life, was listening to his Word. We would, indeed, like to know more about what Jesus said but it is not recorded. What kind of words of Jesus did Mary listen to? The verb in the Gospel — to listen — is in the imperfect tense, meaning that 'she continued to listen' and this would appear to indicate a true teaching on Jesus' part. Did he perhaps speak in parables as he did when addressing the crowds? Most probably not. He would have spoken to Mary as he did to those intimate with him, the Twelve, and some other disciples — a group of fifteen or twenty in all.


### The words of Jesus

The Gospel recounts some of Jesus' sayings which he spoke within the intimate circle of his disciples and which, presumably, he also shared with Mary in Bethany. In the same chapter 10 of Luke we find Jesus calling the disciples to one side and speaking to them: 'Blessed are the eyes that see what you see. For I tell you many prophets and kings desired to see what you see but did not see it, to hear what you hear and did not hear it.' *(v 23)* Up to this point nobody had spoken to Mary about the beauty of her existence, about the blessedness of her state. Listening to the words of Jesus she felt privileged and sensed that these words were important *for her* and not just in themselves. Thinking within herself, she would have said: 'These words are of extraordinary importance for me; never have I thought of such things; I now understand something about myself which is magnificent, splendid and simple.'

The enrichment, the fruitful listening to Jesus, which Mary of Bethany experienced, is one that thrills and engages us because in this act of listening we understand ourselves. It is not a passive act of listening nor is it like notes taken at a lecture. At that moment Mary was actually realising the definition of what it means to be a human.

What, in fact, does it mean to be a man or a woman? It is to discover the mystery of what we are by listening to the Word of one who is greater than ourselves; one who, having created our innermost being, reveals its secrets to us.

Thus Mary of Bethany becomes Mary of Nazareth who, in listening to the Angel Gabriel, understands who God is and what her own role is; or again she becomes the shepherds who, on listening to the heavenly messengers, understand the greatness of God who is in heaven but simultaneously realise that peace is on earth and that this peace is for us.

This is the mystery of every man and woman who sets about seriously listening to the Word: 'I understand you, Lord God, and I understand myself. You reveal yourself to me and you also reveal me to myself.'

Mary, seated at the feet of Jesus, is the perfect example of persons who achieve self-understanding, authenticity and clarity of knowledge through placing themselves in an attitude of listening to the divine Word, a Word which reveals us and at the same time fills us.

The theologian, Karl Rahner, who died recently, entitled his foundational book, *Hearers of the Word:* he wanted to define the human person in terms of the most basic attitude.

The mystery of Mary of Bethany's listening is, therefore, a revelation of our human condition which we are challenged to welcome. Our openness to the Word of God which is free and salvific should teach us that ours is a 'listening existence', a free gift and that we reach fulfilment through generosity.


## Listening and memory

Listening, however, is not complete in the simple act of attending to the proclamation of the Gospel. It is completed and prolonged by our memory which recalls, reflects, coordinates, invites, comprehends and finally discovers the relevance of the Word to me and to my personal life. The Word needs listening and memory in order that the single moments of listening may come together and make sense. Understood in this way memory is basic to an attitude of reconciliation; it is a category essential to our understanding of the person. People grow and become more themselves thanks to memory. This is the characteristic of Mary described by Luke: 'But Mary kept all these things, pondering them in her heart. . . . His mother kept all these things in her heart'. *(Lk 2:19, 51)*

In our English translation the word *'things'* is used. In the original Greek we read 'Mary pondered *"these words"*. . . .'

What words? The words of the shepherds when they found Jesus, or the words spoken by Jesus in the temple? The English translation — 'things' — is justified because the original Greek text means by 'words' either what is said, or the event along with its meaning. Mary lived the memory of the events and their meaning: she showed the ability to interpret the whole thread of her life through repeatedly calling to mind words and events; she thus 'heard' the story of her life as a divine communication about her and upon her.

From Nazareth to the cross Mary continued to remember, to meditate in her heart, and this enabled her to reach a higher level of understanding — God's plan for her and for all humanity.

We must, then, honestly face the fact that the only way to avoid frustration, the feeling of the haphazardness of life, the sense of being a cog in the machine, of being of no significance and without identity, is through listening perseveringly to the Word. In this listening, prolonged by memory and meditation, the events of our lives are part of God's communication in which, like Mary of Bethany, we discover our real importance, our destiny and our own greatness, which surpasses that of those prophets and kings who desired to see and did not see, who desired to touch and did not touch. All of this is given to us through our baptism and through our personal calling as Christians.

I would like to read from a letter which I received some time ago. The letter is from a young woman and, among other things, she writes: 'I need your advice most urgently. I am at this moment in my bedroom and have your photograph on my table in front of me. Do you know I don't recognise myself any more; I don't know how old I am; I don't know if it is true that my name is Betty and that I am so many years of age. Why? I really feel down. I cannot manage a smile; I am afraid of my surroundings, I am afraid of silence. Why? Please answer me — very urgently.'

What we have said up to this might be an answer to her questions. If, in fact, we ask ourselves what Gospel image corresponds to what I have quoted from the letter — a person living through a period of fear and distress, no longer able to smile, no longer sure of her identity — we might think of Martha. Martha is distressed, anxious, tense, unsure, impatient, aggressive, harsh and biting. In fact she shows irritation and harshness towards Jesus himself. Having lost her ability to listen Martha has lost the meaning of her anxiety.

Listening to the word of God is the rock on which our certainty is built: 'You, O God, are the rock of my salvation.'

The good news lies in the fact that this Word exists for me; I can listen to it here and now, in this community, in this cathedral. In making an effort to listen I am being nourished, I grow in faith, in certainty, and together with so many others we grow as the Body of Christ in history.

In this way we become the Church and the Word of Jesus is addressed to us: 'This better part will not be taken from you.' The words of Jesus addressed to Peter are equally addressed to us. 'The gates of hell shall not prevail against it (the Church)' because it is built on the rock of the Word and of listening. Or we can recall the house built on a rock, 'the winds and the rain cannot destroy it'.

## Questions for us

If we want to know if we are really able to listen to the Word, we might ask ourselves:

— During what period of the day do I seriously listen to the Word? Perhaps at the celebration of the Eurcharist during the readings? Perhaps during the moments of silent eucharistic adoration or communal listening? What are my true moments of listening?

— In this our group, do we listen to each other, do we pay attention to each other?

— As engaged couples, do we listen to each other or do we pretend to listen in order to take our turn at speaking?

— Do I know how to make myself heard? This is important. From time to time we hear people say, 'no one listens to me'. But they do not ask if they know how to be heard, if they know the ways of truth necessary to the exercise of this fundamental right of being heard.

— Do I use my memory to prolong the act of listening, so essential if I am to understand the meaning of a series of events? Do I know how to apply what I understand to my life? How do I apply it to the current social situation: for example, to the very serious problems of work, employment and unemployment of young people? If we are really listening then we can integrate all the elements, past, present and future and thus reach a judgement involving commitment that will enable us to advance these important social questions. In relation to peace, do I bring to bear my capacity to listen and to remember the facts, to retain a perspective on history, to reflect on events, carefully sifting through detailed analyses, and thus come to a serious, mature judgment?

— Are listening and memory the basis of my responsible and reasonable activity, present also in my political and other civic commitments?

Grant, Lord, that we may be worthy of that beatitude which you proclaimed to a woman who rejoiced in motherhood; when you said that above and beyond that blessing there is the beatitude of those who listen to the Word and keep it. You expressed a fruitful richness for every person, one which will be the fulfilment of all our lives and which is born of our listening to your Word in a practical way.

Lord, we need to be as you wish us to be. Grant, through the intercession of Mary your mother, that we follow this path.

# 4

# CELEBRATION

# CELEBRATION

*(Exodus 15:19-21)*
*For when the horses of Pharaoh with his chariots and his horsemen went into the sea, the Lord brought back the waters of the sea upon them; but the people of Israel walked on dry ground in the midst of the sea. Then Miriam, the prophetess, the sister of Aaron, took a timbrel in her hand; and all the women went out after her with timbrels and dancing. And Miriam sang to them:*

*'Sing to the Lord, for he has triumphed gloriously;*
*the horse and his rider he has thrown into the sea.'*

*(Luke 1:46-50)*
*And Mary said,*
*'My soul magnifies the Lord,*
*and my Spirit rejoices in God my Saviour,*
*for he has regarded the low estate of his handmaiden.*
*For behold, henceforth all generations will call me blessed;*
*for he who is mighty has done great things for me,*
*and holy is his name.*
*And his mercy is on those who fear him, from generation to*
    *generation.'*

This evening I would like to talk about celebration as an attitude of reconciliation, as an instrument and expression of reconciliation. It may not appear very opportune to speak of celebration during Lent, but in fact the season of Lent is a preparation for the celebration of all celebrations, Easter. We note, therefore, that celebration is at the heart of Christianity; the rhythm of our lives as Christians develops around the high

39

point of the year's celebration, the mystery of Easter; celebration is of the very essence of the Christian's view of the world.

The Old Testament also has a rhythm of celebration: the feasts of Tabernacles, of Dedication and of Pentecost. Biblical celebration is composed of wonder, joy, gratitude, rejoicing and praise. These realities are all present in the ancient hymn of victory and celebration which is read in chapter 15 of the Book of Exodus: it is a hymn of the saved, a hymn of the crossing of the Red Sea; it is a baptismal hymn *par excellence*.

Recalling what we said at an earlier meeting we will be immediately aware that celebration arises from seeing God's practicality as he works in history and therefore presupposes our *listening* to God's wonderful works. Seeing the divine practicality gives rise to rejoicing; our joy bursts forth because God is so great in our midst.

From the Christian's point of view the source of this outburst of joy is our experience of the Passover of Jesus; for the Hebrews in the Old Testament it was the coming out of Egypt and the crossing of the Red Sea. In both cases the experience is that of reconciliation, the celebration of God's reconciliation with us and of us among ourselves.

Nevertheless it is difficult to speak about celebration; we find it much easier to talk about suffering, malaise, tiredness and boredom, for these appear to be our lot much more frequently. Celebration, strangely, can seem tiresome, excessive and indefinable: there comes quite an agonising point that forces upon us attitudes that do not really correspond to what we feel deep inside ourselves. We should, then, approach this subject with delicacy, with clarity, with lucidity and limit ourselves to giving hints and suggesting questions.

## The hymn of the prophetess Miriam and the hymn of Mary of Nazareth

The hymn placed on the lips of Miriam, sister of Moses and Aaron, is only nine words long in the original Hebrew. However, as they succeed each other, these nine words give the impression of extraordinary rejoicing.

The longer canticle of Moses, which we read, appears rather to be a more ample version of the two short lines, 'Sing to the Lord, for he has triumphed gloriously. The horse and his rider he has thrown into the sea'.

The Lord is mighty and he has granted victory. Miriam is called a prophetess because of her ability to interpret the mystery of God, present in history. She sees the practicality of the divine mystery and so is capable of expressing human amazement at the mystery of salvation becoming historical and practical.

She sings her hymn while dancing in front of the women of the community and the chorus of women respond with timbrels and dance in a circle. From that moment her words, a human expression of amazement at the marvels of God, have become part of the history of Israel.

There is a passage from traditional Hebrew writing that may well help us to understand the strength and the style of this hymn:

> The entire posterity of Abraham was inhabited by the breath of God through the joy of this hymn. When freed from exile Jacob did not sing a hymn; nor did Isaac when spared from the knife. Abraham did not sing when liberated from the furnace; but on that day, not only Moses the prophet and Miram the prophetess sang, but every man and woman in Israel from the elderly to the newborn, all sang. Those still in their mother's womb sang for at that moment the glory of the eternal was seen more clearly than by Ezekiel in the hour of his glory.

Instinctively we are inclined to apply this reading from the *Talmud* to the hymn of Mary of Nazareth at the sound of which the child in Elizabeth's womb leapt for joy. This marks the all-pervasiveness of biblical celebration, the way in which all involved are gathered almost contagiously into the celebration. This, then, is the importance of the short hymn from Exodus, chapter 15. It reminds us of other ancient hymns — Deborah's in chapter 5 of Judges and the canticle of Jephthah's daughter, again in Judges. These are examples of the ability of the people of God to give expression to their common joy through the words of some inspired women — themselves living images of the soul of Israel.

Who, then, is this Mary of Nazareth who sings the Magnificat? She is the soul of Israel; she is the whole people; all its people, she is humanity to which she gives a voice; she is humanity both humbled and surprised by God's practical tenderness, she is poor and suffering humanity, that humanity about which Sister Christina[1] spoke to us recently. She is all humanity surprised by God's tenderness, and attentive to God's actions on its behalf.

Mary, therefore, is the paragon of humanity's celebration. In her we discover that delicacy, care, clarity and lucidity, which are the hallmarks of celebration.

In Mary we discover that ability to understand what really gives joy to the world, what really transforms history into an act of rejoicing in God. In savouring her words we understand what a people in celebration really means. It is a people who recognises in amazement the greatness of the God who looks on the poor, who looks on nothingness and out of it creates a strong and powerful people, a source of strength, beauty and truth.

'Mary, we ask you to make us understand the power of your hymn and to question ourselves on the basis of these two hymns.' Are we a people who know how to celebrate according to the words of the psalms: 'Blessed are those who know how to rejoice'?

Is it not true that our celebrations are often artificial, that our Sundays are monotonous and lifeless? Is it not also true, perhaps, that the major annual celebrations of the Church — Christmas, Easter and Pentecost — are cluttered with many things, but with no room for rejoicing?

### An experience — and a testimony

I would like to describe an experience and introduce a testimony. I had the experience a few days ago. I was bound for Acireale for a meeting of the dioceses of Sicily, and due to air traffic problems arrived very late. I arrived in the hotel well after midnight only to find a large number of delegates (about 1,500) still in the convention hall, discussing, chatting amicably to each

---

1. Sister Christina, who works in San Vittore Prison, had previously spoken to the group of her experience.

other and all in a calm and tranquil manner. I must confess that a feeling of great joy came over me: I thought to myself, these are people who are happy to be together, people who know how to celebrate together. And then I thought how nice it would be if the next meeting of all the dioceses of Italy could express, apart from the usual formulae, a joy in being willingly together. This experience brought back to me the many similar experiences I had in the various parishes during my pastoral visits where, in all simplicity, we had moments of joy and genuine community celebration.

Now I would like to introduce a piece of testimony from the pages of *Manzoni* (today, in fact, is the bicentenary of his birth),[2] which shows how the simple joys of ordinary people almost contagiously bear fruits of reconciliation.

The Unnamed [*l'Innominato*] had spent a night full of thoughts, anxieties, terror and delirium:

> And, lo! about break of day, a few moments after Lucia had fallen asleep, while he was seated motionless in his bed, a floating and confused murmur reached his ear, bringing with it something joyous and festive in its sound. Assuming a listening posture, he distinguished a distant chiming of bells; and, giving still more attention, could hear the mountain echo, every now and then, languidly repeating the harmony, and mingling itself with it. Immediately afterwards his ear caught another, and still nearer peal: then another, and another — What rejoicings are these? What are they all so merry about? What is their cause of gladness? — He sprang from his bed of thorns; and, half dressing himself in haste, went to the window, threw up the sash, and looked out.

Manzoni then goes on to describe the slow advance of the crowds at dawn. They came from all sides, from all the valleys, all heading towards one place. He continues:

2. Manzoni, A., *I Promessi Sposi* (The Betrothed Lovers) English edition, The Minerva Library of Famous Books, Ward, Lock and Co., London, New York and Melbourne, 1889 — pp. 245-246.

What the — is the matter with these people? What cause of merriment can there be in this cursed neighbourhood? — And calling a trusted fellow who slept in the adjoining room, he asked him what was the cause of this movement. The man replied that he knew no more than his master, but would go directly to make inquiry. The Signor remained with his eyes riveted upon the moving spectacle, which increasing day rendered every moment more distinct. He watched crowds pass by, and new crowds constantly appear; men, women, children, in groups, in couples, or alone; one, overtaking another who was before him, walked in company with him; another, just leaving his door, accompanied the first he fell in with by the way; and so they proceeded together, like friends in a preconcerted journey. Their behaviour evidently indicated a common haste and joy; and the unharmonious, but simultaneous burst of the different chimes, some more, some less contiguous and distinct, seemed, so to say, the common voice of these gestures, and a supplement to the words which could not reach him from below. He looked and looked, till he felt more than common curiosity to know what could communicate so unanimous a will, so general a festivity, to so many different people.

As we know, this experience of celebration led the Unknown to Archbishop Frederick Borromeo and eventually to conversion. It was a celebration that drew people who at first were opposed to it, almost indeed cursing it; then gradually they were involved in it themselves.

## Questions for us
The *first question* might be:
— What, for me, have been the best celebrations?
I can answer the question without any hesitation. Without any doubt the most beautiful celebrations which I experienced were during those meetings I had with prisoners in gaol. They were for me moments of simplicity, of real serenity and deep humanity.

The *second question:*

— Do we know how to celebrate together, how to open our hearts in shared joy?

The *third question:*

— Can we make God's celebrations ours?

Sister Christina has already quoted the basic biblical texts: 'Rejoice and be glad, for this your brother was dead and has returned to life; he was lost and is found.' These are God's celebrations. And there is another statement in the New Testament: 'There is more joy (celebration) in heaven for the return of one sinner than for the ninety-nine who have no need for penance.'

Do I know how to celebrate God's feasts — am I capable of being an instrument of reconciliation? In a society which is increasingly contentious, where, even among Christians, the rule of 'an eye for an eye and a tooth for a tooth' seems to hold sway, what can I do? In a society which is so pre-occupied with defence and counter-attack, what can I do? Are we capable of giving expression to celebrations of reconciliation when a brother returns to the fold?

Let this be our preparation for Easter. We will live the Easter mystery of reconciliation to the extent that we are capable of celebrating God's celebration, capable of welcoming with open arms those who return and pardoning all those who may have offended us.

# 5
# TENDERNESS

# TENDERNESS

*(Luke 7:11-15)*
*Soon afterward he went to the city called Nain and his disciples and a great crowd went with him. As he drew near to the gate of the city, behold a man who had died was being carried out, the only son of his mother, and she was a widow; and a large crowd from the city was with her. And when the Lord saw her, he had compassion on her and said to her, 'Do not weep'. And he came and touched the bier and the bearers stood still. And he said, 'Young man, I say to you, arise'. And the dead man sat up, and began to speak. And he gave him to his mother.*

*(John 20: 11-18)*
*But Mary stood weeping outside the tomb, and as she wept she stooped to look into the tomb; and she saw two angels in white, sitting where the body of Jesus had lain, one at the head and one at the feet. They said to her 'Woman, why are you weeping?' She said to them, 'Because they have taken away my Lord, and I do not know where they have laid him'. Saying this, she turned round and saw Jesus standing, but she did not know that it was Jesus. Jesus said to her, 'Woman why are you weeping? Whom do you seek?' Supposing him to be the gardener, she said to him, 'Sir, if you have carried him away, tell me where you have laid him, and I will take him away'. Jesus said to her, 'Mary'. She turned and said to him in Hebrew 'Rabboni!' (which means Teacher). Jesus said to her, 'Do not hold me, for I have not yet ascended to the Father, but go to my brethren and say to them, I am ascending to my Father, and your Father, to my God and to your God.' Mary Magdalene went and said to the disciples, 'I have seen the Lord'; and she told them that he had said these things to her.*

When, last October, I was thinking about themes for these meetings, and I noted tenderness, little did I realise the maze

49

of problems involved in this vast theme, one which nevertheless has important repercussions on our daily lives. In fact the topic touched on what is central to all human and religious communication, and to all interpersonal and social relations.

Little wonder, then, that I feel the need to ask the help of Our Lady of Tenderness, who is represented on the twelfth century eastern icon known as Vladimirskaja. You can admire this icon at the right of the altar while I read out a description of it: 'The hands have noticeably long fingers and they caress the child who is clothed in a gold coloured garment. Mother and child are cheek to cheek in an attitude of deep tenderness and protection. The child's face is fixed in contemplation on the mother's. The artist sacrificed proportion between the figures in order to emphasise the mutual love between them. One arm, which is surprisingly long, goes around the mother's head and rests delicately on her neck, indicating a strong and tender embrace. The other arm rests trustingly on Mary's shoulder.' Here we have an image of tenderness, mutual tenderness, the closeness of the presence, indeed the immanence of the divine in Christ for humanity. Let us pray:

> Mary, mother of tenderness, grant us the grace not only to understand and explain what tenderness is, but to live it. Soften our hardened hearts; bend and make sincere our minds and our hearts and make them simple.

Let us also ask the intercession of those who once were here with us, but now are no longer on this earth. A few days ago I got a letter telling me about Albino. On 7 February Albino was at our meeting. He went home happy and enthusiastic, looking forward to attending our subsequent meetings. Alas, he was not able. On 20 February a severe headache forced him to return home from school. An incurable disease was diagnosed and on 28 February he closed his eyes to the life he loved so much. The writer of the letter added, 'I have heard that the Thursday meetings have given rise to various kinds of vocations: among these I would like to include the call that came to Albino.'

Together with you I would like to pray to him and to all those other witnesses now with God, that they may help us in our reflection.

## Examples of tenderness

How are we to define the relationship of tenderness with faith, with the Gospel, with love, with the cross, with the body and the senses, with tears and with death?

Various examples spring to mind. We all know the case of John XXIII. On the evening of 11 October — the day of the opening of Vatican II — speaking from the window of his apartment, he said to the people assembled in St Peter's Square, 'When you return home, give your children a hug, tell them it's a hug from the Pope'. Those of us who heard these words were somewhat dismayed, not knowing what connection there could be between them and the Council. It was only later that we realised that they were indeed the right words, words of tenderness.

Another example is taken from the life of St Thérèse of Lisieux. In her autobiography she describes her relationship with an old, slightly grouchy nun rejoicing in the name Sister St Peter. She writes: 'Every evening when Sister St Peter began to shake her hour-glass I knew then it was time to go. It is unbelievable how upsetting, especially at the beginning, this move was for me: however, I always started immediately and a whole ceremony began. Her stool had to be moved in a certain way, slowly and carefully . . . then she had to be followed and held onto by her cincture. I did this as gently as I could but if, by any mishap, she made a false move she immediately claimed that I wasn't holding her properly and that she was about to fall. "Dear God, you're going too quickly, you'll kill me!" Then if I went a bit more slowly — "Watch out, keep up with me." I don't feel your hand on me, you've let me go, I'm falling; I always said you were too young." And then when we reached the dining room there were further complications. She had to be helped to sit down, but carefully in order not to hurt her; then her sleeves had to be rolled up and this again in a certain way. Then I was free and I could leave. With her poor crippled hands she arranged her bread in the bowl as best she could. I noticed this, and then every evening before leaving her I used to arrange this for her. As she had not asked me to do this she was quite moved by my thoughtfulness and, even though I had not intended it that way, through this little service, I got into her good books and especially (as I learned later), because when I had finished cutting her bread for her I always gave her one of my nicest smiles before I left.'

We find a further image of tenderness in Bernanos' book, *The Diary of a Country Priest,* when he says that 'grace' consists of forgetting oneself. 'But if all traces of pride were dead in us, then the great grace would consist in loving ourselves humbly as we would any other suffering member of the body of Christ.' It seems to me that in this passage we find the true measure of tenderness.

A final example of tenderness is St Francis of Assisi in the first words of his *Testament.* 'The Lord granted me, brother Francis, the grace to do penance because when I lived a sinful life I found the sight of lepers too repugnant'. (I have just returned from Brazil where I saw and met very many lepers.) The Lord himself led me among them and I treated them with care and when I left them, what previously seemed repugnant, became sweet to my body and soul.'

## Tenderness

We have gathered together a few examples of tenderness, each one differing somewhat from the others. We will now try to describe tenderness itself. Tenderness is love that is respectful, discreet, practical, attentive, joyful — all themes on which we have meditated during previous meetings. Tenderness is tangible love, open to reciprocity, not mean, not grasping, not pretentious, not possessive, but strong in its own weakness, efficacious and victorious, disarmed and disarming.

I realise how hard it is to define tenderness and admit that I have strung together a number of adjectives; yet if we grasp something essential and important about it, we will realise that tenderness is always an ingredient of all human communication.

## Gospel passages

Where do we discover tenderness in the Gospel passages which we have quoted?

In the passage from Luke (7:11-15), dealing with the widow from Nain, tenderness is expressed not only in the words 'young man, I say to you, arise'. This is certainly an extraordinary gesture of love but the tenderness is found in the words 'I do not weep'. We are reminded of the actions and heart of the Good Samaritan: 'He saw him and was moved'. Or again we think of the leper in Mark (1:41): 'Jesus saw him and, moved with compassion, he touched him.'

In the passage from John (20:11-18) there is tenderness in the way Jesus presents himself to Mary of Magdala. At the outset he says, 'Woman, why are you weeping?'. He then says to her, 'Mary'. It has the whole force of a personal address, an approach to an individual person. It is not a big proclamation: just her name, but said in a special way.

And there is another word of tenderness — 'Do not hold me' — which I would like to explain using the words of a woman writer. 'The Gospel does not present women and their tenderness in that negative suspect way which we find in traditional interpretations. An example of this latter is the picture by Giotto in the Scrovegni Chapel (Padua) which shows a marked reluctance on the part of Jesus at Mary's gesture — here we have the influence of the Latin translation, 'Noli me tangere' (Do not touch me). . . . It is not tenderness that it being rejected, nor a gesture of tenderness that is being forbidden. The tender gesture that sees the person in the actual touching, that touches with respect and with an admission of his mystery and his otherness — this gesture is contrasted with the scene of a different and untender touching by Thomas (Jn 20:25) who wants to touch the wounds of Jesus as if he were an object. His touching is not condemned; it is tolerated, but Jesus points out its futility. In contrast, Jn 20:17 is not a refusal, but rather an invitation to tenderness: to be tender in the very act of tenderness and not hold Jesus back. We are not to seek our relationship with Jesus by holding on to him as though he were a hostage, nor by grasping a figure when there are much greater demands made on us; we are to consume his flesh and blood, that is, to allow ourselves to be assumed in him (not, therefore, holding him for ourselves); we are to allow ourselves to be transformed by him and to be obedient to the spirit of his life ('God and say to my brethren'). In the case of Mary of Magdala her touching would be wrong if it were a holding on to Jesus and not an acceptance of him as alive and going to the Father. In our case, we touch him as the living one who is the basis of communion, fraternity, service and going forth, and who rejects separation, possessiveness and privilege, that is to say, untenderness.

## Hardness of heart

At this point it would be useful to reflect on the opposite to tenderness. It is hardness of heart, mind and spirit, it is cultural narrowness, ideological closedness and rigidity in all its forms. We know that hardness of heart is one of the most insidious enemies of Christ and of Christianity. It is frequently condemned in the Gospel as calcifying, as making hearts of stone, and as closing the mind. Jesus is saddened at the Pharisees' hardness of heart and he looks on them with indignation. Indeed it was because of hardness of heart among his people that Moses had to compromise on the question of marital fidelity.

The risen Jesus rebukes his disciples for their hardness of heart which was tied up with their slowness to believe; they are rebuked because they are foolish and slow to believe. In the Acts we read that it was those who were hard and uncircumcised of heart who stoned Stephen to death. Lack of tenderness, rigidity, tends towards cruelty.

## The roots of hardness of heart

What is the cause of rigidity? What shuts out real tenderness? There are three causes: fear, lack of moderation and a false idea of God.

First of all, *fear:* fear of oneself, fear of exposing ourselves, fear of the other person, fear of reciprocal relationships. Fear of reciprocity is at the root of all forms of paternalism and of explicit or implicit possessiveness of others. It produces an inability to enter into genuine dialogue, an inability to take an active part in group activity; it produces a need always to be in control out of fear of what others might say.

The second cause of rigidity is *lack of moderation* which leads, on the one hand to sugary, even ridiculous sentimentality, on the other hand to sensuality, inordinate greed and possessiveness.

*A false idea of God* is probably also at the root of fear, greed, possessiveness and immoderation. We spoke of a false idea of God during last year's session when we reflected on the *Miserere.* The question we raised was: Do we have a false idea of God? A false idea of God will, in fact, give a certain falsity to all our relationships. For example, is it possible that one who sees God as all-powerful and despotic, i.e. lacking in tenderness, could have a proper image of Mary and could describe her well? What would emerge would be a caricature or blur, even if the author did not intend this.

If our idea of God is a violent being who imposes his will as inexorable laws, we can never understand tenderness, much less live it in our relations with God and with others. We will never grasp the great manifestations of God's tenderness in Mary and in the infant Jesus.

The counter-measures to fear, immoderation and a false idea of God are *discipline, courage* and *contemplation.* Tenderness involves discipline, even bodily discipline: discipline of the eyes, of the heart and renunciation of sensual greed. Tenderness involves courage, the courage to take small steps, to make small affective investments (a smile, a word, a good wish, an expression of thanks, a greeting, a phrase: here is the paper . . . I will make you a cup of coffee . . . have the TV channel you want . . .). There is wisdom in these small gestures which constitute the web of our daily existence. There is prudence and courage in proceeding with even the smallest affective gestures for there is always an element of risk. We are never certain how we will be received — guardedly or openly. Tenderness is risk. Tenderness demands contemplation, that silence which brings us into experiences of respect for God, for others, for nature, for things. Tenderness is nourished through such contemplation.

## Questions for us

We have endeavoured to understand tenderness. We have read about it in the two passages from the Gospel. We have queried the opposite to tenderness and looked for the root causes of hardness of heart. I would now like to propose four questions which you can ask yourselves as you think about the icon of Our Lady of Tenderness and consider Jesus before the widow of Nain and Mary of Magdala.

1. What does tenderness mean for me? In the concept which I have of it do I recognise those attitudes which we discovered in Mary, in Jesus, in the saints?

2. Is this attitude a constant in my life?

3. Is it a genuine authentic attitude or are there pseudo-imitations of genuine tenderness? Is there greed in my life that is masquerading as tenderness, is self-interest passed off as tenderness, do I cloak vengefulness and possessiveness in the garb of tenderness?

4. What part do obstacles to tenderness play in my life: fear, lack of discipline and moderation, a false idea of God, lack of contemplation?

> Mary, Mother of tenderness, grant that we may not only know these things but also interiorise them. Grant that we may live these realities and not just think we have them within us. Grant that we may be more concerned with others than with ourselves as we contemplate you and your Son.

# 6
# GIVING

# GIVING

*(Luke 7: 36-50)*
*One of the Pharisees asked him to eat with him, and he went into the Pharisee's house, and sat at table. And behold, a woman of the city, who was a sinner, when she learned that he was sitting at table in the Pharisee's house, brought an alabaster flask of ointment, and standing behind him at his feet, weeping, she began to wet his feet with her tears, and wiped them with the hair of her head, and kissed his feet, and anointed them with the ointment.*

*Now when the Pharisee who had invited him saw it, he said to himself, 'If this man were a prophet, he would have known who and what sort of woman this is who is touching him, for she is a sinner'. And Jesus answering said to him 'Simon, I have something to say to you'. And he answered, 'what is it, Teacher?' 'A certain creditor had two debtors; one owed five hundred denarii and the other fifty. When they could not pay, he forgave them both. Now which of them will love him more?'*

*Simon answered, 'The one, I suppose, to whom he forgave more'. And he said to him, 'You have judged rightly'. Then turning towards the woman he said to Simon, 'Do you see this woman? I entered your house, you gave me no water for my feet, but she has wet my feet with her tears and wiped them with her hair. You gave me no kiss, but from the time I came in she has not ceased to kiss my feet. You did not anoint my head with oil, but she has anointed my feet with ointment. Therefore I tell you, her sins, which are many, are forgiven, for she loved much; but he who is forgiven little loves little'. And he said to her 'Your sins are forgiven'. Then those who were at the table with him began to say among themselves, 'Who is this, who even forgives sins?' And he said to the woman, 'Your faith has saved you; go in peace'.*

*(Jn 19:25-27)*
*But standing by the cross of Jesus were his mother, and his mother's sister, Mary the wife of Clopas, and Mary Magdalene. When Jesus saw his mother, and the disciple whom he loved standing near, he said to his mother, 'Woman, behold, your son!' Then he said to the disciple, 'Behold, your mother!' And from that the disciple took her to his own home.*

We will devote our final meeting to the key theme of *gift*. We could also use the word 'gratuitousness' or, indeed, the words of Jesus as recalled by Paul in the Acts. 'There is more joy in giving than in receiving' *(20:35)*. The definition of man as given in the Council document *Gaudium et spes (Constitution on the Church in the Modern World)* might equally constitute our starting point: 'man is created by giving himself.' These are all valid expressions of the reality before which we place ourselves this evening, trusting in God's help and the grace of the Holy Spirit.


**The gospel texts**
In the text from Luke's gospel Jesus is presented not as teaching directly but in an ordinary everyday situation. We are not given, as it were, a well-arranged portrait but rather a live snapshot. Taken somewhat by surprise Jesus reacts almost instinctively — says out what he feels. In fact, one of the great values of this text is that it gives us an insight into the spontaneous actions of Jesus.

John's gospel recalls some of Jesus' last words on the cross, as it approaches the culminating point of the Fourth Gospel: Jesus transfixed, from whose side flows blood and water. It is quite likely that the contemplation of this mysterious event gave rise to the entire gospel of John.

In a certain sense our text is the penultimate revelation of Jesus. The gospel has described the crucifixion and the division of the garments by the soldiers. It recalls the fulfilment of the prophetic verse of the Psalm: 'They have divided my garments among them and for my tunic they cast lots' and concludes 'the soldiers did this' *(Jn 19:23-25)*, wishing to underline their cruelty, their cynicism and their greed.

Then he gives a totally different reaction. But standing by the

60

cross of Jesus were his mother, her sister Mary of Clophas, Mary of Magdala and John.

The words which Jesus pronounces are uttered in a situation of absolute truth, in his moment of extreme agony when a man utters only what is nearest his heart, what he must say at all costs.

## Whoever loves gives all

Our reading of the two texts suggests four successive reflections on our theme of giving.

### Whoever loves gives what they have

The woman who goes to Simon's house has three things: her ointment, her aromatic oils and her ability to be attentive. With great simplicity she gives all she has without thinking too much about it. In return, Jesus gives her respect, he is attentive to her, he judges her favourably and, in a difficult situation, accepts her. There is an exchange of gifts: both give spontaneously what they have there and then.

A gift is active, it is something done, not something thought about. It brings about reality. On the cross Jesus has nothing more to give and yet he sees the disciple whom he loves and who is still too young to carry on alone. John still needs to be cared for, he needs to be helped and Jesus gives him his own mother. And to his mother, who is now on her own, he gives John. This is how Jesus expresses the reality of gift at the great final moment of his life.

To give means to communicate what we have, whether it is little or much, without even asking ourselves whether it is little or much. It should be enough for us to be able to give what we have.

### Whoever loves considers others more important

A second reflection may help us further to understand the idea of exchanging. *A gift is a declaration of importance.* In both texts — John and Luke — we discover that behind the gift and an integral part of it is the fact that the other person is deemed more important than oneself. The woman who goes to Simon's house considers Jesus more important than her own reputation; her own convenience takes second place; she goes beyond self-interest and expresses her love in an action that arouses astonishment. Jesus looks on the woman, considers her dignity, the truth of her actions; he deems her more important than the onlookers who were looking for gratification from him and would have criticised him; he exposes himself without thinking of the others.

The gift enters deeply into the mystery of the human person. It cannot even be understood by ordinary standards because it is expressed in gestures which can, on occasion, appear strange and almost foolish.

## Pardon

There comes, then, a time when giving reaches its perfection. The gift is totally gratuitous, unmerited, and creates such an imbalance between the giver and the receiver that it almost defies thought and imagination. The word which best expresses this absolute gift is *pardon*. Pardon is such a gratuitous gift that it goes beyond and transcends what one can receive or merit. Pardon is a most perfect gift. It is the gift which Jesus offers the woman. 'Your sins are forgiven — your faith has saved you.'

Pardon is the gift which Jesus, in his act of supreme self-sacrifice, offers from the cross to humanity: a sinful humanity is now welcomed as sons and daughters.

For this reason the cross is the unequivocal sign of totally gratuitous love, the supreme and inexhaustible exemplification of pardon. The saints never tire of contemplating the crucifix, the mystery of God's perfect gift, the mystery of pardon offered to sinful humanity, the gift of reconciliation.

## Pardon creates givers

Jesus, turning to Simon, said of the woman: 'Her many sins have been forgiven for she has loved much.' These mysterious words are rich in meaning but above all they indicate this truth: our consciousness of being forgiven creates an ability to give.

I would like to read to you a few verses from a poem that may help us in our contemplation of these words of Jesus. The poem was given to me today by a group of prisoners with whom I had lunch. The prison is in this diocese and is remarkable for the fact that there are no prison bars. About seventy, mostly young people, are held in detention while engaged in an educational work programme. They are now serving out the last months of their sentences and because they are committed to rehabilitation the questions that arose during our conversations had a certain urgency. They asked: 'Will we really be pardoned? Will we be welcomed back into society?'

The poem which they gave me expresses very well the strength of a person who, even in the most difficult of situations, looks for love, who even in the most unpromising surroundings of the prison is looking for gratituous acts of giving. The title of the poem is 'A Bit of Heaven' and it begins:

> I made this my piece of heaven
> Ploughed it with a sunbeam
> And sowed it with seeds of love. . .

It goes on to explain how this undertaking runs into difficulty:

> And bird song ceases suddenly
> The white clouds are swept away
> And sombre ones draw near.

> One tear falls
> It swells to a great lament
> In desperation I call on you O Lord.

The final part brings us back again to hope and peace:

> I plough a new furrow with a sunbeam
> I sow again with seeds of love
> I give thanks to you O Lord.

## Questions for us

I would like us to reflect on the following questions:

1. *Is there such a thing as a gift?* Not just the little gifts that we exchange, but real gifts, gratuitous giving, genuine disinterestedness. Does real gift exist in our world? We are inclined to base judgements on our own experience: when we receive signs of affection we are inclined to affirm the existence of the gratuitous, of disinterestedness, of gift. More often, however, on looking around us, we are led to believe that everything is calculated, is just egoism if not downright hooliganism and wickedness. There are incidents that strike us as being gratuitous violence and would lead us to believe that there is no gratuitous good, that no one acts in a disinterested fashion, that no one manages to do good in a spontaneous way without some hope of a return. If we ourselves remain disillusioned when our gift is not understood or accepted, this simply means that deep down we too expect some return. These are, perhaps, depressing thoughts that might lead us to believe that the genuinely gratuitous does not exist and that if God is gratuitous then he does not exist either! This gives added importance to our question: does the gratuitous really exist? We should learn, however, to distinguish lest we fall into the trap of the kind of reasoning that I have described, into which I too risk falling from time to time. We must acquire spiritual and mental discernment. There are, indeed, situations in which gratuitous gift is absent, and such situations are many.

On the other hand there are situations in which gratuitous gift — perhaps not as a determining factor — is nonetheless present, and they are certainly frequent.

Then finally, there are the rarer cases in which pure gratuitousness is the determining factor. It is not the whole activity but it is the cause of the action and is the criterion by which action is measured. There will always be some degree of reward, a certain degree of satisfaction, or self-gratification but this does not take from the fact that gratuitousness is decisive in the activity. We are unjust when we condemn an action where the decisive factor is gratuitousness even though something shabby or egoistical remains. Perhaps we close our eyes to the core of the action, the gratuitousness, and we dwell over-critically, indeed cynically, on the marginal — the elements of selfishness or mediocrity. I think, for example, of the way many initiatives taken by the Church or by Christian communities are regarded.

I must agree that true gratuitousness is rare, but actions that have gratuitousness as their determining factor can be found and ought to be accepted as such.

Thus our question might be more specific: are there initiatives that are purely gratuitous? I believe there are very few. Jesus on the cross, the eucharist, martyrdom, are the models which should inspire us so that even in our weakness we may undertake initiatives which, through God's grace, will be determined mainly by gratuitousness.

Thus, I would try to answer the first question by trying to grasp clearly what God does in the world by his love, what the world, in fact, is, and what our place is in this world.

2. *What do I receive as a gift?* This question should clarify for us what it is we receive as a gift. In fact many of my most authentic attitudes result from my astonishment at the gifts I receive. Banality and mediocrity are born of lack of astonishment.

3. *What do I give that is truly gratuitous?* What can I genuinely give as a total gift? I am on the wrong road if I do not part with some essentials, freely and gratuitously.

> Lord, what can I give that I may be like you, that I may be in you and in your truth, that I may be inspired by your Spirit?

**Conclusion**
At the end of our fifth year of meetings to study the Word of God together here in the cathedral we are called to share with others what we have learned. This is no small responsibility. Catholic action groups are already looking for ways of spreading the gift of our meetings. Much will depend on each one of you,

who have lived the experience of shared gift. One person's silence becomes a gift to another, one person's listening becomes a gift to another. There will be risks involved in trying to give expression to your shared experience of listening to the Word of God. It will not be enough to set up programmes to spread it. You will need to recreate that climate of relevant and devout listening, an awareness of the power of the Word when heard in silence. This is the principal gift which the Lord has granted us. Let us place ourselves before the Word in the certain knowledge that if we listen and assimilate it in silence it is for us life and strength, it is the presence of Christ and a gift for our brothers and sisters.

'Mary, you who are the woman of reconciliation, guide us along the paths of truth: grant that we may be able to give what we received as a free gift; help us to understand the direction in which the Spirit of your son Jesus is leading the Church; put in our hearts and in our mouths the hymn of gratitude and praise of the Father from whom all things come and to whom all return.'